COOL CRAFTS FOR KIDS

TISSUE PAPER CREATIONS

Jane Yates

WINDMILL
BOOKS™

Published in 2017 by **Windmill Books**, an Imprint of Rosen Publishing
29 East 21st Street, New York, NY 10010

Developed and produced for Rosen by BlueAppleWorks Inc.

Creative Director: Melissa McClellan
Managing Editor for BlueAppleWorks: Melissa McClellan
Designer: T.J. Choleva
Photo Research: Jane Reid
Editor: Kelly Spence
Craft Artisans: Jerrie McClellan (p. 12, 20, 22, 24, 26, 28); Jane Yates (p. 8, 10, 14, 16, 18)

Photo Credits: Cover middle Mike Flippo/Shutterstock; cover left Real Deal Photo/Shutterstock;
cover right Syda Productions/Shutterstock; title page background Diane C Macdonald/Shutterstock;
title page Austen Photography; TOC Elena Elisseeva/Shutterstock; page tops, back cover bottom
Lyudmila Suvorova/Shutterstock; p. 4 top left kontur-vid/Shutterstock; p. 4 top right antpkr/Thinkstock;
p. 4 bottom leftMilleflore Images/Shutterstock; p. 4 bottom right Vlad Ozerov/Shutterstock; p. 5 top
Marcie Fowler - Shining Hope Images/Shutterstock; p. 5 left to right and top to bottom: Michael
Kraus/Shutterstock; Crackerclips/Dreamstime.com; Alexandr Makarov/Shutterstock; Darinina/
Shutterstock; tudioNeosiam/Shutterstock; Samantha Roberts/Shutterstock; Picsfive/Shutterstock; p. 7
bottom hobbit/Shutterstock; p. 30 left Hut Hanna/Shutterstock; p. 31 bottom EsSueno/Shutterstock;
p. 6 – 29, back cover top, back cover middle Austen Photography

Cataloging-in-Publication Data
Names: Yates, Jane.
Title: Tissue paper creations / Jane Yates.
Description: New York : Windmill Books, 2017. | Series: Cool crafts for kids | Includes index.
Identifiers: ISBN 9781499482409 (pbk.) | ISBN 9781499482416 (library bound) |
 ISBN 9781508192848 (6 pack)
Subjects: LCSH: Paper work--Juvenile literature. | Tissue paper--Juvenile literature. |
 Handicraft--Juvenile literature.
Classification: LCC TT870.Y38 2017 | DDC 745.54--dc23

Manufactured in the United States of America
CPSIA Compliance Information: Batch #BW17PK:
For Further Information contact Rosen Publishing, New York, New York at 1-800-237-9932

CONTENTS

it lets you see where you need to go.

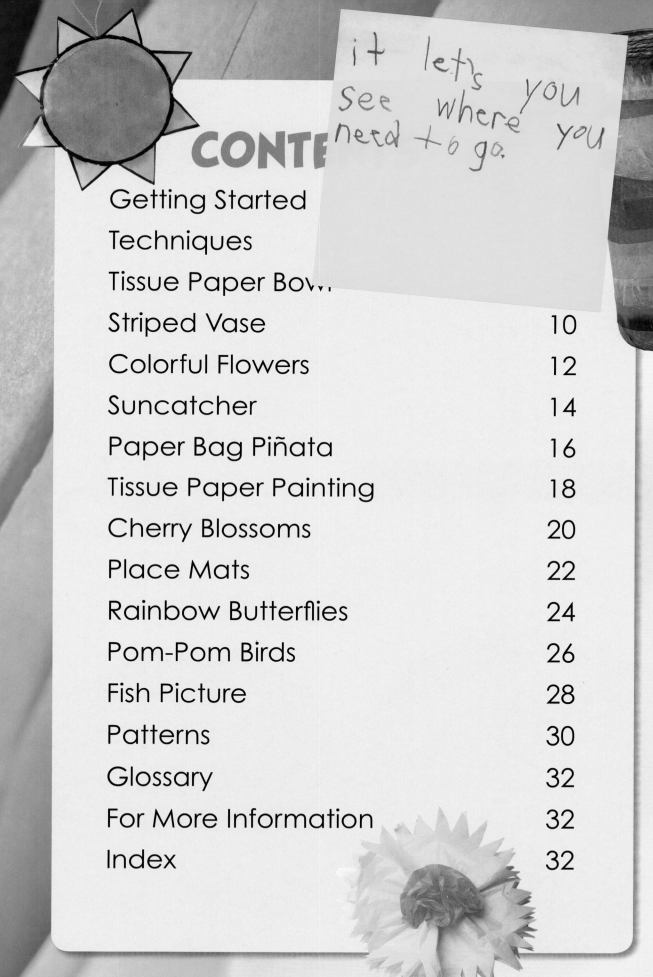

GETTING STARTED

Tissue paper can be used for more than just wrapping presents! This colorful paper is thin and translucent, which mean it allows some light to pass through it. Sheets of tissue paper come in a variety of colors and patterns. It is perfect for making fun crafts!

You can recycle leftover tissue paper that was used to wrap gifts. New tissue paper can also be purchased in card shops or in the gift wrap section of stores. Bleeding tissue paper and other supplies can be purchased at a craft store or dollar store. Once you have what you need, organize your supplies in boxes or plastic bins. Then they are ready to use whenever you want to create tissue paper crafts.

RULER

SCISSORS

TISSUE PAPER

Regular - Colors will not bleed when wet

BLEEDING TISSUE PAPER

Bleeding - The colors will bleed when wet

Did You Know?

Paper was invented in China thousands of years ago. Over time, different kinds of paper were created. Tissue paper was originally **manufactured** to wrap **fragile** items for shipping. Soon, people began using the colorful sheets to wrap gifts. Today it is also used to make colorful crafts!

PAINTER'S TAPE

GLUE

GLUE STICK

PAPER

STRING

PENCIL

HOLE PUNCH

A note about measurements

Measurements are given in US format with metric in parentheses. The metric conversion is rounded to make it easier to measure.

TECHNIQUES

Have fun while making your tissue paper crafts! Be creative. Your projects do not have to look just like the ones in this book. You can use whatever colors, shapes, and patterns that you want. If you don't have a certain material, think of something similar you could use. For crafts that need a pattern, you can use the patterns on pages 30 and 31, or you can draw your own. Use the following techniques to create your tissue paper crafts.

PAPER-MACHE GLUE

- Add equal amounts of white glue and water in a bowl. Mix the glue and water together with a spoon. If you have leftover glue, put it in a container with a lid (An empty yogurt container works well) and use it later.

USING PATTERNS

- Patterns help you cut out exact shapes when making crafts.

- Use tape or pins to attach the pattern to the paper before you start cutting.

- When cutting out a shape, cut around the shape first, then make smaller cuts.

- When cutting with scissors, move the piece of paper instead of the scissors.

- Make sure you keep your fingers out of the way while cutting. Ask an adult for help if needed.

Trace the pattern.

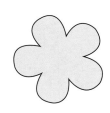
Cut the pattern out.

Place the pattern on the tissue paper.

Cut the tissue paper along the pattern lines.

CUTTING OUT CIRCLES

● Cut out a square piece of tissue paper. Cut each corner off, then trim around the edges until you are pleased with the shape.

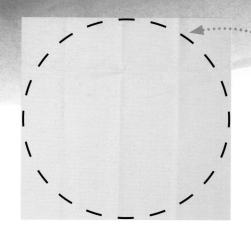

MAKING FLOWER STEMS

● Take one sheet of newspaper or craft paper. Cut it to the desired length, then tightly roll the paper into a tube. Wrap tape around the tube to hold it shut. Then completely tape over the stem with green painter's tape.

ACCORDION FOLD

● Fold an edge of the paper over to the width you want. Firmly press along the fold to crease it.

● Flip the paper over so that the first fold is at the bottom and faces down on the work surface.

1 2 3 4 5 6

● Fold the folded edge up until all of it is on the top surface. Line up the original edge of the paper with the new edge, then crease the new fold.

● Continue folding in increments until all of the paper is folded and creased.

CREASING TISSUE PAPER

● Make a fold, then rub your fingers along the edge to make a crease.

Handle tissue paper with care—it tears easily!

7

TISSUE PAPER BOWL

You'll Need:

- ✔ Tray covered in wax paper or cardboard to work on
- ✔ Bowl
- ✔ Plastic wrap
- ✔ Tissue paper
- ✔ Scissors
- ✔ Glue
- ✔ Foam brush

1 Cover the outside of the bowl with plastic wrap. Place the bowl upside down on a tray or cardboard.

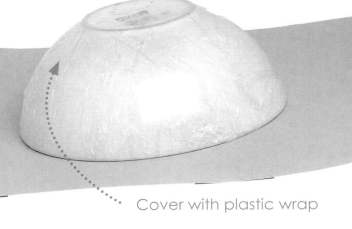

Cover with plastic wrap

Tear strips

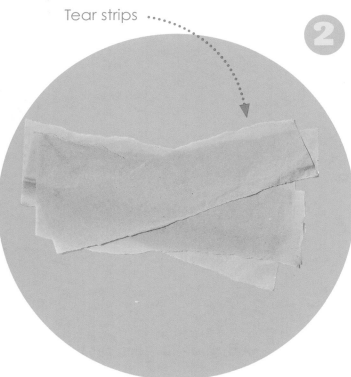

2 Tear strips of orange tissue paper about 1 inch (2.5 cm) wide. The strips need to be long enough to cover the bowl.

3 Prepare the paper-mache glue in a container. Brush the glue on the strips.

Apply glue

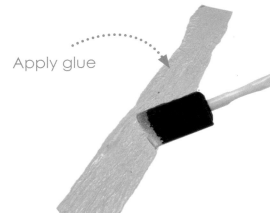

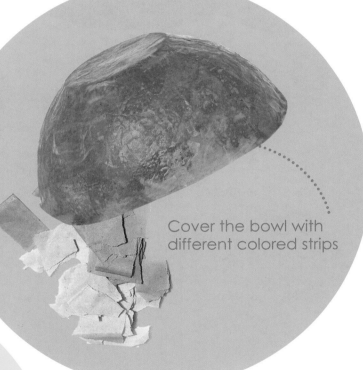

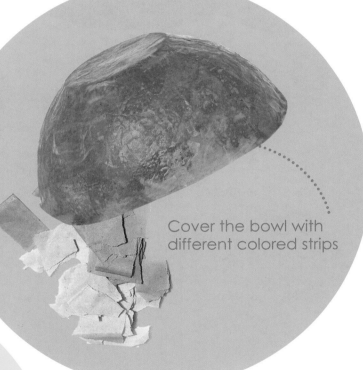
Lay the strip glue side down on the bowl

4 For the first layer, lay a tissue strip on the bowl, placing the glue side down. Use your fingers to smooth out any creases. Continue overlapping strips until the bowl is covered. Let it dry.

5 For the second layer, tear strips out of blue tissue paper. Brush the strips with glue, then lay each strip on the bowl. Continue until the bowl is covered. Leave it to dry.

Cover the bowl with different colored strips

Trim the edges

6 Remove the bowl by pulling out the plastic wrap. Carefully peel the plastic wrap away from the tissue paper. Trim the edges of the bowl with scissors.

STRIPED VASE

You'll Need:

✔ A clean, empty bottle or jar (glass or plastic)
✔ Tissue paper
✔ Scissors
✔ Paper-mache glue
✔ Brush
✔ String or yarn

1 Using different colors, cut several narrow strips of tissue paper. The strips need to be long enough to wrap around the bottle.

2 Prepare your paper-mache glue.

3 Brush glue onto the bottle. Wrap strips of tissue paper around the bottle.

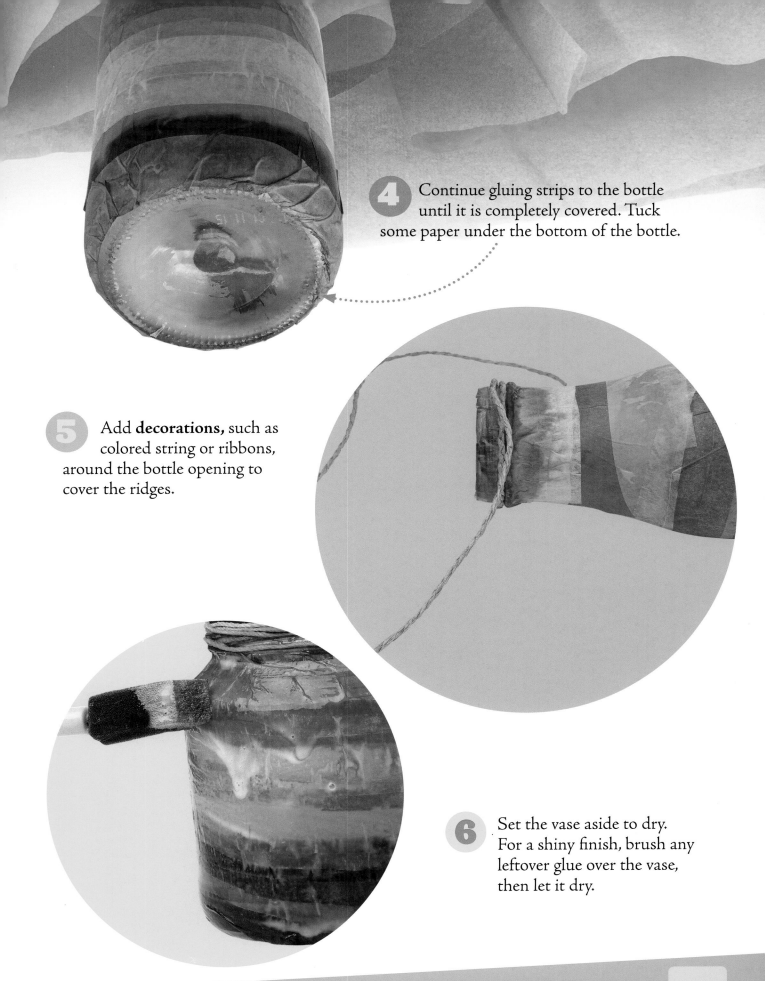

4 Continue gluing strips to the bottle until it is completely covered. Tuck some paper under the bottom of the bottle.

5 Add **decorations,** such as colored string or ribbons, around the bottle opening to cover the ridges.

6 Set the vase aside to dry. For a shiny finish, brush any leftover glue over the vase, then let it dry.

COLORFUL FLOWERS

You'll Need:

- ✔ Five sheets of yellow tissue paper
- ✔ Two sheets of orange tissue paper
- ✔ Scissors
- ✔ One piece of craft paper to work on
- ✔ Green painter's tape

1 Stack together the five sheets of yellow tissue paper. Cut them into a circle.

2 Fold the stack in half. Cut out triangle shapes around the edge. Unfold the stack and lay it flat.

3 Cut four smaller circles out of orange tissue paper. Place the circles on top of the yellow tissue paper.

4 Gather the centers of the circles around the eraser end of a pencil. Scrunch the paper together, then remove the pencil. Wrap green painter's tape around the scrunched end.

5 Attach the flower to a stem (see page 7) by taping the gathered point to the stem.

6 Fluff up the petals by carefully separating the layers.

SUNCATCHER

You'll Need:

- ✔ Tracing paper
- ✔ A clear plastic sheet
- ✔ Marker
- ✔ Scissors
- ✔ Tissue paper
- ✔ Glue
- ✔ String
- ✔ Tape

1 Trace the pattern pieces on page 31 onto a piece of tracing paper.

2 Using the pattern as a guide, transfer the pattern onto a sheet of clear plastic with a black marker.

3 Cut out several small squares using yellow and orange tissue paper.

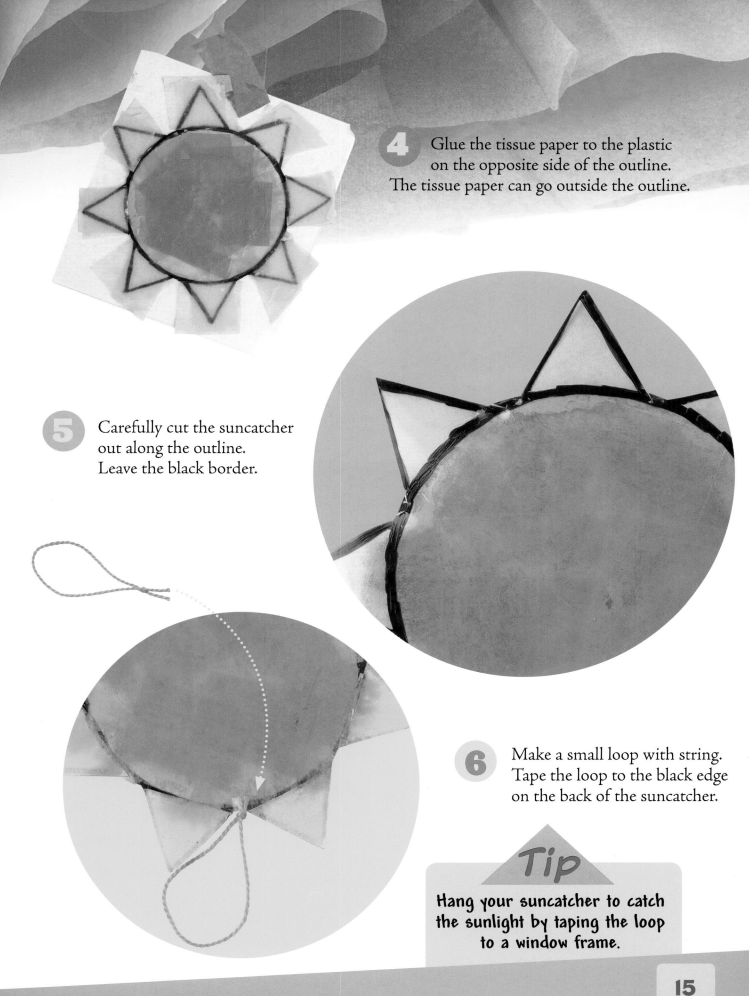

4 Glue the tissue paper to the plastic on the opposite side of the outline. The tissue paper can go outside the outline.

5 Carefully cut the suncatcher out along the outline. Leave the black border.

6 Make a small loop with string. Tape the loop to the black edge on the back of the suncatcher.

Tip

Hang your suncatcher to catch the sunlight by taping the loop to a window frame.

PAPER BAG PIÑATA

You'll Need:
- ✔ Tissue paper
- ✔ Scissors
- ✔ Paper bag
- ✔ Hole punch
- ✔ Glue stick
- ✔ String

1 Cut several strips using different colors of tissue paper. The strips should be the length of the bag and 1½ inches (4 cm) wide.

2 Use scissors to cut fringe along one edge of each strip.

3 Fold the top of the paper bag over on itself, leaving about a 1-inch (2.5 cm) flap. Punch a hole through both layers.

4 Cut a piece of the strip that is the width of the bag. Rub the glue stick along the top of the fringe. Starting at the bottom, stick strips onto the bag.

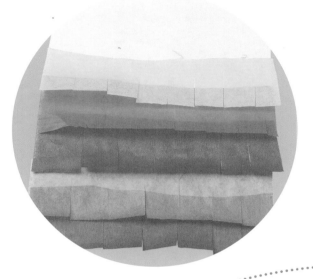

5 Layer each strip over the last, until one side of the bag is covered. The fringe should overlap each layer. Repeat this step for the back and sides of the bag.

6 Fill the bag with candy. Punch a hole through the tissue paper in the same place as the first hole. Fold a piece of string in half and push the loop through the hole. Pull the other two ends of the string though the loop and tighten. You are ready to hang your piñata!

Tip

Use the techniques described above to create a big piñata for a birthday party. Form a donkey-shaped frame out of recycled cardboard and cardboard tubes. Decorate it with tissue paper strips and have fun with it at your party!

TISSUE PAPER PAINTING

You'll Need:

✔ Tracing paper
✔ Scissors
✔ Marker
✔ Watercolor paper
✔ Tissue paper

✔ Cup for water
✔ Paintbrush

1 Trace the pattern pieces on page 30 onto a piece of tracing paper.

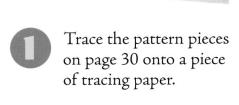

2 Cut out the patterns and use them as a guide to cut shapes out of tissue paper. Cut out a long, thin green stem.

3 Use a paintbrush to cover the paper with water. The paper needs to be damp, but there should not be pools of water.

4 Place the pieces of tissue paper on the wet paper so they form a flower.

5 Cut strips of blue tissue paper. Place the strips along the edges of the paper to make a border. Leave to dry.

6 After everything dries, carefully remove the tissue paper pieces.

Tip

If the paper dries before you finish, brush more water on the paper.

CHERRY BLOSSOMS

You'll Need:

✔ Long, thin branch
✔ Pink tissue paper
✔ Scissors
✔ Pencil
✔ Glue

1 Find a branch that you can use. Make sure it has a few smaller twigs sticking out.

2 Using the pattern on page 30 as a guide, cut out squares from pink tissue paper. You will need two squares for each blossom.

3 Place one square on top of another square at an angle as shown.

4 Place the eraser end of a pencil in the center of the two squares. Gather the tissue around the pencil. Pinch the bottom and remove the pencil. Tightly twist the gathered paper to hold the pieces together.

5 Repeat Steps 3 and 4 for each blossom.

6 To attach the blossoms, place some glue on the branch. Press the twisted part of the tissue blossom into the glue. Repeat for each blossom. Leave to dry.

PLACE MATS

You'll Need:

- ✔ Clear self-adhesive vinyl paper
- ✔ Tissue paper
- ✔ Scissors
- ✔ Colored art paper or poster board

1️⃣ Tear several different colors of tissue paper into squares and rectangles.

2️⃣ Cut or tear some pieces into shapes like flowers and butterflies.

3️⃣ Cut a rectangle of clear self-adhesive vinyl paper. Tape it to your work area.

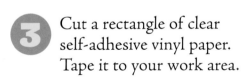

4 Remove the backing. Peel one corner at a time, then replace the tape to hold the mat in place. Start laying the shapes down on the sticky side of the paper.

5 As you work, leave a border around the tissue. Continue covering the mat so there are no gaps.

Craft paper

6 Cut a piece of craft paper that is a bit bigger than the place mat. Place it over the tissue paper side of the mat. Smooth it down. Trim the extra paper away. Cover this side with another piece of clear vinyl to seal the place mat.

RAINBOW BUTTERFLIES

You'll Need:

- ✔ Four pipe cleaners
- ✔ Tissue paper
- ✔ Scissors
- ✔ Glue stick

1 For the upper wings, bend two pipe cleaners into teardrop shapes. Twist the ends together. Leave a short piece sticking out as shown.

2 For the bottom wings, trim 3 inches (7.5 cm) off the other two pipe cleaners. Repeat Step 1 with the bottom wings.

3 Join the two larger wings together by twisting the ends together. The other two ends will be the butterfly's **antennae**.

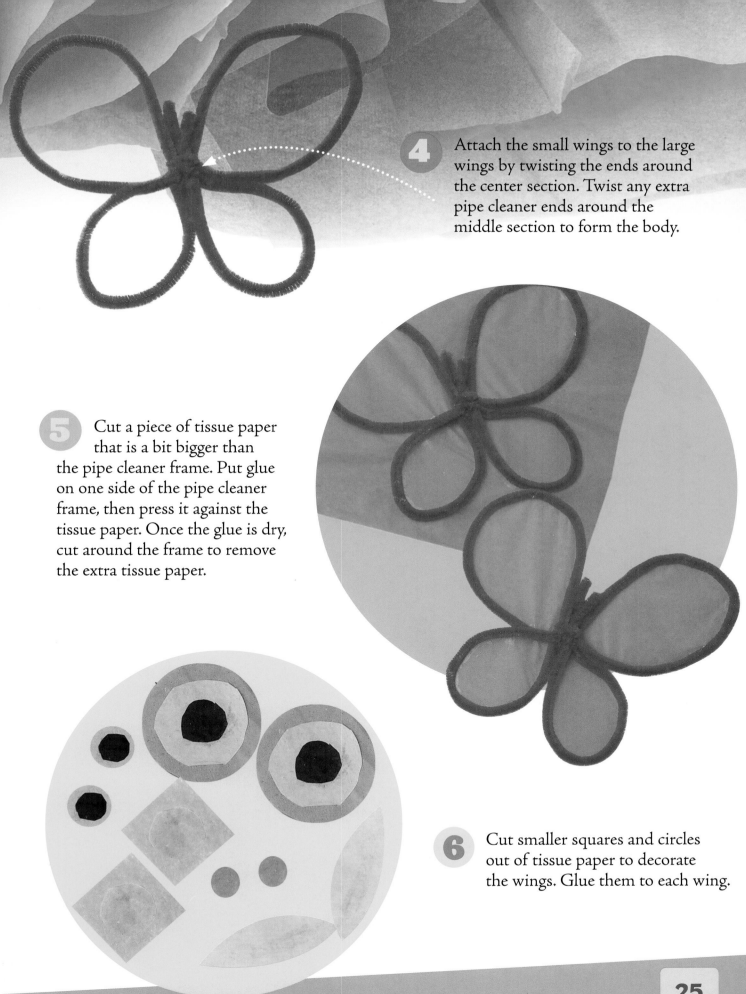

4 Attach the small wings to the large wings by twisting the ends around the center section. Twist any extra pipe cleaner ends around the middle section to form the body.

5 Cut a piece of tissue paper that is a bit bigger than the pipe cleaner frame. Put glue on one side of the pipe cleaner frame, then press it against the tissue paper. Once the glue is dry, cut around the frame to remove the extra tissue paper.

6 Cut smaller squares and circles out of tissue paper to decorate the wings. Glue them to each wing.

POM-POM BIRDS

You'll Need:
- ✔ Five sheets of tissue paper, 6 inches by 14 inches (15 cm by 36 cm)
- ✔ Colored art paper
- ✔ Scissors
- ✔ String
- ✔ Glue stick

1 Stack five sheets of tissue paper on top of each other. Make a 1-inch (2.5 cm) accordion fold along the length of the tissue paper stack. Crease each fold. (See page 7.)

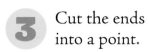

2 Wrap a string tightly around the center of the paper. Make a knot.

3 Cut the ends into a point.

4 Carefully pull apart the layers of tissue paper, one layer at a time.

5 Fluff up the layers and shape them into a ball.

Fluff the layers

6 Cut out eyes, feet, and a beak using the patterns on page 31. Glue together the eyes and beak, then glue all the pieces onto the pom-pom.

Tip

If you want to hang your pom-pom bird, use the long piece of string from Step 2. Otherwise, trim the string after Step 6.

FISH PICTURE

You'll Need:

✔ Tracing paper
✔ Marker
✔ Scissors
✔ White card stock
✔ Tissue paper
✔ Glue stick
✔ Colored pencils or crayons

1 Trace the fin and tail patterns on page 30 onto a sheet of tracing paper. Use the pattern as a guide to draw the pattern on card stock.

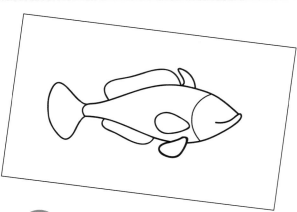

2 Cut out the fins and tail.

3 Cut 1-inch (2.5 cm) strips of tissue paper out of blue, green, and yellow tissue paper. Cut the strips into squares.

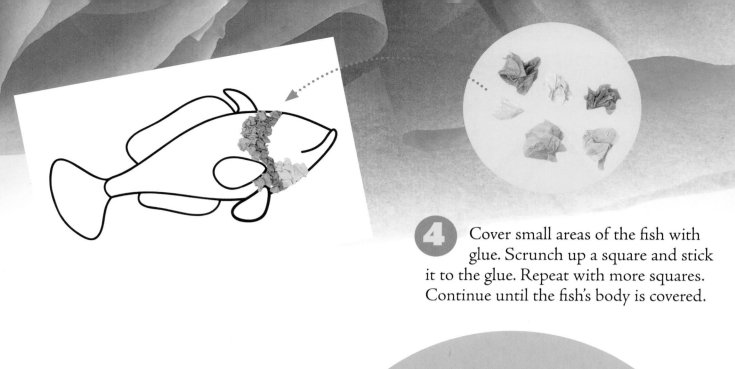

4 Cover small areas of the fish with glue. Scrunch up a square and stick it to the glue. Repeat with more squares. Continue until the fish's body is covered.

5 Use the tail and fin patterns to cut matching pieces of tissue paper. Cut three smaller triangles for the tail. Glue the triangles in layers on top of one another as shown. Cut out small circles for the eyes and glue them together.

6 Glue the fins and tail to the fish at the edges so they stick out a bit. Stick the eye pieces onto the fish's face. Color the background with colored pencils.

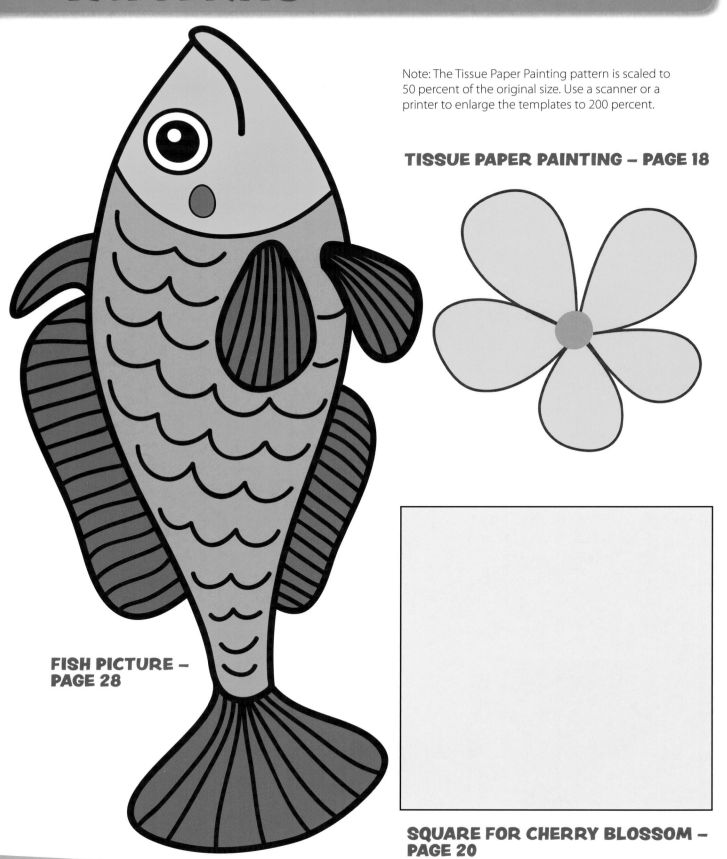

Note: The Tissue Paper Painting pattern is scaled to 50 percent of the original size. Use a scanner or a printer to enlarge the templates to 200 percent.

TISSUE PAPER PAINTING — PAGE 18

FISH PICTURE — PAGE 28

SQUARE FOR CHERRY BLOSSOM — PAGE 20

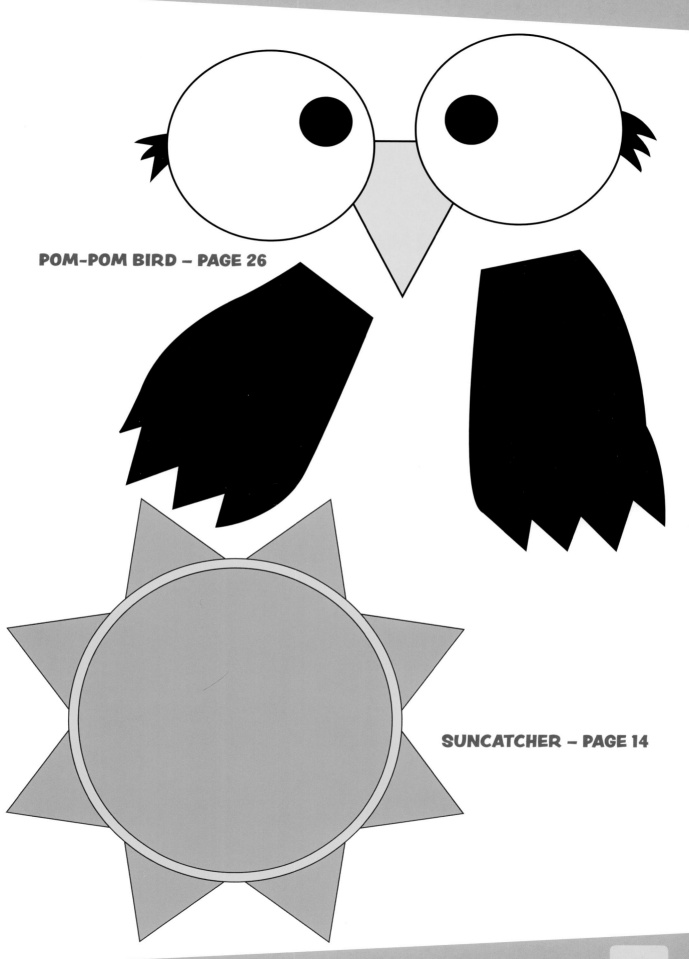

POM-POM BIRD – PAGE 26

SUNCATCHER – PAGE 14

GLOSSARY

antennae Long body parts used to sense things found on the heads of most insects.

decorations Something that is added to something else to make it prettier.

fragile Easily breaks.

manufactured Made, produced.

FOR MORE INFORMATION

FURTHER READING

Burke, Judy. *Look What You Can Make With Paper Bags.*
Honesdale, PA: Highlights Press, 2013.

Castleforte, Brian. *Papertoy Monsters: 50 Cool Papertoys You Can Make Yourself!*
New York: Workman Publishing Company, 2010.

Petelinsek, Kathleen. *Crafting with Tissue Paper.*
North Mankato, MN: Cherry Lake Publishing, 2014.

WEBSITES

For web resources related to the subject of this book, go to:
www.windmillbooks.com/weblinks and select this book's title.

INDEX